DIVE INTO SPACE SCIENCE!!

PBC

Copyright © P B C
All Rights Reserved.

This book has been published with all efforts taken to make the material error-free after the consent of the author. However, the author and the publisher do not assume and hereby disclaim any liability to any party for any loss, damage, or disruption caused by errors or omissions, whether such errors or omissions result from negligence, accident, or any other cause.

While every effort has been made to avoid any mistake or omission, this publication is being sold on the condition and understanding that neither the author nor the publishers or printers would be liable in any manner to any person by reason of any mistake or omission in this publication or for any action taken or omitted to be taken or advice rendered or accepted on the basis of this work. For any defect in printing or binding the publishers will be liable only to replace the defective copy by another copy of this work then available.

To Someone Special

Contents

Foreword

The author of the book, PBC is an aspiring amateur scientist who is around the age of 14-15. He has a passion for writing books for young adults and for them to understand complex topics and ideas simply and interestingly.

CHAPTER ONE

Stellar Classification

Stellar classification or star classification is a way to identify different stars based on their spectral lines. Spectral lines are observed by the person who works in the field related by passing the electromagnetic radiation of the star through a prism to create lines of colors that are similar to that of a rainbow. Each line indicates the element that the star has. Stellar classification also helps us understand different stars' mass, size, temperature, and certain things about them. This is mainly used to estimate or understand stars beyond our solar system or stars which are found beyond our planet.

Types of stars:

As we know, there are billions of quadrillions of stars in our milky way alone. Because of this, we have created a stellar classification. These stellar classifications based on the Morgan Keenan system are as follows:

Class O type: The type of stars in this category are very hot and very luminous. They are very very scarce in the galaxy. We can say that these stars are about 1 in 3,000,000 of the stars found in the galaxy.

Class B-type: The type of stars in this category are very luminous and bluish. They have a relatively short lifespan and exhaust much more quickly than the other types of stars.

Class A-type: The type of stars in this category are very common and can be seen with our naked eyes at night. These stars are white or bluish-white.

Class F-type: The type of stars in this category are yellowish-white in color. This type of star is almost 3% of the stars found in the Milky way galaxy.

Class G-type: The type of stars in this category are yellow, orange, or sometimes red. Even our Sun is classified in this category (G2V).

Class K-type: The type of stars in this category is slightly cooler than G-type stars and have similar orangish colors.

Class M-type: The type of star in this category is the most common in the whole universe and they are the coolest star type that has been found yet. The class M-type is almost 76% of the stars in the universe.

Other types of stars in the same form of the system:

1. Class D-type: white dwarfs

2. Class S and C-type: Carbon stars

The classification above which I mentioned was based on their spectral lines and their luminosity. The other way to classify different types of stars is through their sizes. They are as follows:

1. Hyper giants

2. Supergiants

3. Normal giants

4. Dwarfs

5. Sub-dwarfs

This system by which a star is classified based on the size of the star. Example: As per this system, we can classify our Sun as a normal giant and we can classify Proxima Centauri as a dwarf star (Red dwarf). Here is a table that can tell you about the Morgan Keenan system clearly:

O type: 30,000 K - Blue

B type: 10,000 K - 30,000 K - Blue-white or Deep blue white

A type: 7,500 K - 10,000 K - White or Blue white

F type: 6,000 K - 7,500 K - Yellow white or white

G type: 5,200 K - 6,000 K - Yellow or yellowish-white

K type: 3,700 K - 5,200 K - Light orange or Pale yellow-orange

M type: 2,400 K - 3,700 K - Orange-red or Light orange-red

- Carbon stars: Carbon stars or class C-type stars are luminous red giants which have more carbon dioxide than oxygen in their atmosphere. These stars are scarcely found in outer space. The temperature of these stars ranges from 5100 K to 2600 K. These stars are also very small in size as compared to other stars like our Sun. Some of these stars have similar sizes to Jupiter and Saturn.
- White dwarf stars: White dwarf stars are stellar core remnants. This type of star is very dense and its mass is similar to our Sun. As for now, our Milky Way galaxy contains around ten billion white dwarfs. Some of these types of stars are Sirius B (Nearest White dwarf to our Sun), Stein 2051 B, Procyon B, etc. The average temperature of these stars is from 10,000 kelvin to 100,000 kelvin.
- Neutron stars: Neutron stars are the collapsed core of a supermassive star. The temperature of the surface of these stars is unimaginable. The temperature of these stars is around 1,000,000 celsius compared to our Sun's average temperature (5,600 to 6,000 Celsius). This type of star is also very dangerous as they have a very strong magnetic field, which is much stronger than our planet's magnetic field. Let's say that Earth has a magnetic field of 0.00005 teslas, black and a neutron star's magnetic field is 100,000,000,000 tesla. The nearest neutron star to our solar system is 500 light-years away.

(Note: Tesla is the SI unit for identifying an object's magnetic field)

There are different and infinite amounts of stars that we can find soon. If we are lucky enough to pass the great filter, we may someday explore the vast universe and learn more about it. We could even find new stars and planets which are way beyond our understanding. But, for the time being, we can see any star within our grasp thanks to our billion-dollar telescopes, which we launched into space on massive space rockets.

(Fun Fact: Solar superstorms can cause black-outs all over the world in seconds)

Black holes and white holes

As we see through our telescopes in outer space, we can see things that we can imagine and things that we can not imagine seeing. Two of these unimaginable things are black holes and white holes. Black holes are the region of space, where gravity is so strong that anything that comes near it never gets out, even light. Whereas white holes are the region of space, where gravity is also strong, white holes don't attract things or pull them, but they push or exert things out of them. Even black holes and white holes have different types, shapes, sizes, masses, and gravitational fields. The temperature of black holes is estimated to be almost zero degrees from the inside and immensely hot from the hot side. As said by a person, "everything that once lived has to die one day or the other". This same thing applies to black holes, white holes, and objects which are powered by some other things. Black holes and white holes die as soon as the energy they use is exhausted or completely gone. They evaporate into space as soon as the energy they use is depleted. As for now, we can estimate there are as many as 1 billion black holes in our galaxy. These black holes which are in our galaxy range from a few solar masses to millions and billions of times the mass of our star (Sun).

Illustration of a Black Hole

White holes: As we all know, black holes take or attract matter or anything in it and that thing never comes back out. But in 1964, a Russian cosmologist, Igor Novikov, predicted white holes. White holes are exactly the opposite of black holes. Black holes suck objects inside of them, but white holes exert objects, matter, and energy out of them. White holes are yet to be detected by anyone in this world as till now we have only gotten to know about the existence of black holes in 1974 and 1971 with the help of radio telescopes and recently in 2017, scientists had finally taken an image of a black hole called M87 in the center of a galaxy called Messier 87 but till now the existence of a white hole is still a mystery. Either this thing could be hypothetical in the future or a thing that exists along with black holes.

Illustration of a White Hole

Types of black holes:

1. Stellar black holes: This type of black hole is formed due to the gravitational collapse of a star. These black holes are also known as collapsars.
2. Intermediate black holes: This type of black hole is mostly found near huge star and space object clusters. These black holes also have much more mass than stellar black holes.
3. Supermassive black holes: This type of black hole is the largest black hole type we could ever imagine. This type of black hole has a mass of millions to a billion times the mass of our Sun. These black holes are formed due to gravitational collapse which is far too powerful.
4. Miniature black holes: Miniature black holes or micro-black holes are types of black holes that are very small compared to the rest of the 3 types of black holes. This type of black hole was first introduced by Stephen Hawking in 1971. This type of black hole may or may not be as it is not yet confirmed.

White holes: As we all know, black holes take or attract matter or anything in it and that thing never comes back out. But in 1964, a Russian cosmologist, Igor Novikov, predicted white holes. White holes are exactly the opposite of black holes. Black holes suck objects inside of them, but white holes exert objects, matter, and energy out of them.

Parts of a black hole:

1. Singularity: Singularity is the inestimable point at the center of a black hole where all matter, objects, or things collapse. Everything like matter or things that have passed through the Event Horizon ends up here. At this point (singularity) gravity is infinitely strong, or I can say that gravity is much more powerful than any astronomical object. Even light cannot escape a black hole as black holes suck everything in it and even light. Due to this, it is quite hard to locate a black hole without predictions or precision of the region of space where a black hole is most likely to be found.

2. Event Horizon: The event horizon is the boundary or the perimeter between the black hole and the vacuum of space. It is the place where all matter and things that enter it get pulled in. Everything which passes this boundary or perimeter gets sucked into the black hole and never comes out.

3. Hawking Radiation: Hawking radiation is small quantum particles that appear at the event horizon and steal its (Blackhole's) mass away. This is also the main reason for the black holes' end or evaporation in space.

4. Ergosphere: Ergosphere is the region around the boundary of the black hole (Event horizon) where it is not possible to stay properly or to stay still. This is caused because of the super-fast rotation of the black hole. The speed of the rotation of the black hole is unimaginable and incomprehensible.

5. Accretion disk: This is the area near the black hole that contains very hot gases and dust particles, which orbit at unimaginable high speeds around the black hole. Some particles/objects

ejected from the white hole become trapped in the accretion disk in this region.

Parts of white hole:

1. Singularity: Singularity is the inestimable point at the center of a white hole where all matter, objects, or things exerts. Everything inside the singularity, such as matter or things, radiates out through the event horizon. At this point (singularity) gravity is infinitely strong, or I can say that gravity is much more powerful than any astronomical object.
2. Event Horizon: The event horizon is the boundary or the perimeter between the white hole and the vacuum of space. It is the place where all matter and things get out or are pushed out into outer space. In this part of the white hole, all matter and things that the white hole exerts come out from here into the vacuum of space.
3. Hawking Radiation: Hawking radiation is small quantum particles that appear at the event horizon and steal its (white hole's) mass away. This is also the main reason for the white holes' end or evaporation in space.
4. Ergosphere: Ergosphere is the region around the boundary of the white hole (Event horizon) where it is not possible to stay properly or to stay still. This is caused because of the super-fast rotation of the white hole. The speed of the rotation of the black hole is unimaginable and incomprehensible.
5. Accretion disk: This is the area near the black hole that contains very hot gases and dust particles, which orbit at unimaginable high speeds around the black hole. Some particles/objects that were exerted from the white hole get stuck right in the accretion disk for this area.

CHAPTER THREE

Wormholes

Wormholes are 3 to 4-dimensional objects in space, which bend space-time and make any two points much faster to travel. What do I mean by dimensions you ask? Well dimensions are of 0, 1, 2, 3 and 4. 0 Dimension is a single point or well just a dot for instance. 1 Dimension is a line which has a length and 2 Dimensions is like a 2d shape like square or rectangle, which has both lengths as well as a height. Guess what 3 dimensions might have? 3 Dimensions have length, height, as well as breadth, and examples of 3-dimensional objects can be cubes, cuboids, spheres, etc. The reality in which we all live is currently 3-dimensional in our observation as we can move front and back, left and right, and up and down if we have a ladder. Examples of 4-dimensional objects are tesseract, sprinter, glome, etc. 4 Dimensions was a term which was made into use by Einstein in his theory of general relativity, called Spacetime, and later on, 4 dimensions were put into use for defining other things as well. Spacetime in general is the combination of Space which is 3 dimensional and time which is 1 dimensional as we can only move front and back in time or well only front in time for now as cannot go back in time and 3 dimensional for space as we can move in all 3 different coordinates (x,y and z axis) of points in space. The spacetime will be later explained in another chapter so let's continue with wormholes.

As for now, wormholes exist theoretically but till now we haven't yet spotted or detected any sort of wormhole that might exist in the universe or in any observable region of space that we currently know of. To make you understand what wormholes are, let us say that we have two points in space, Point A and Point B:

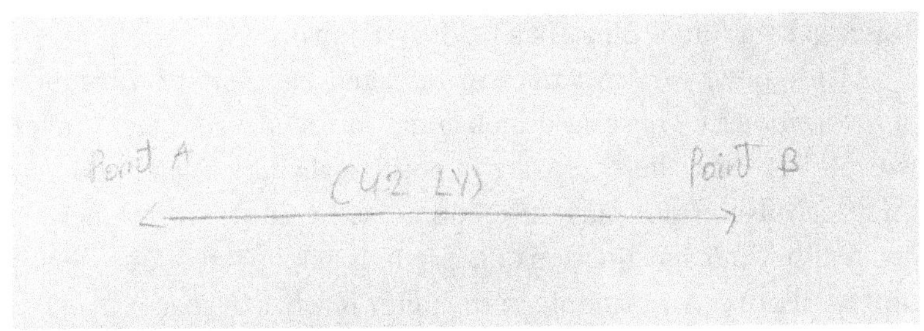

Distance = 4.2 LY (Light years)

In this image, we can see that the distance between point A and point B is 4.2 light-years away, which is too far compared to the distance between us (Earth) and Neptune. In this, we can say that we have to travel in a straight line or in the straightest way possible.

Now, what if I bend this straight path or line or curve this line at 90 degrees:

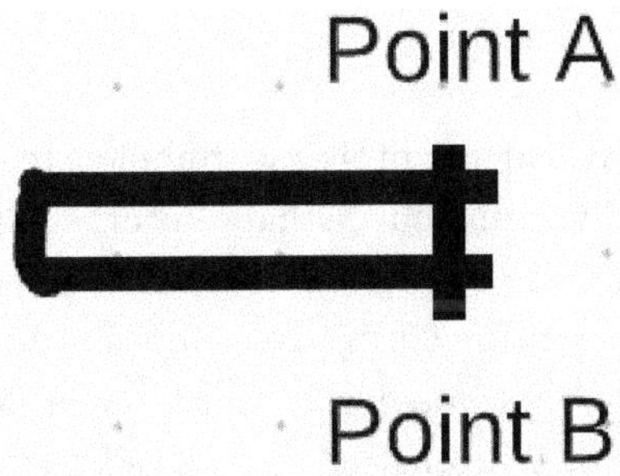

Distance = few kilometers or millions of kilometers

In this, we can observe that the distances between the points have reduced from light-years (LY) to a couple of meters or kilometers.

Similarly, wormholes are objects which curve or bend space to make two points easier to access (Access here means to travel) instead of traveling hundreds of light-years. This object is based on a special solution of Einstein's field equations.

As for now, we have not yet detected any sort of wormhole or wormholes. These 4-dimensional objects like black holes, wormholes, white holes, etc are hypothetical and we can not detect them because of our current technology. In short, wormholes are not real but our imaginations on Earth, for now. But soon, we will find or discover a wormhole in the outer reaches of space.

As per scientists, wormholes can enable us to travel at a speed faster than light inside the wormhole. Some people also say that wormholes can also enable us to travel in time, but this theory is uncertain and very hypothetical. In me, we can travel in the future because of the differences in time while traveling in a wormhole and staying on Earth. We can also say that while traveling in a wormhole, time dilation occurs. Wormholes are also said to enable us to travel to a different universe, far beyond our reach with our current technology.

Out of these wormholes, the most fascinating and real wormhole concept is the Einstein-Rosen bridge or the Schwarzschild wormhole.

Einstein-Rosen bridge: This is a wormhole named after two great people, Albert Einstein and Nathan Rosen. In the 20th century (1935), both Einstein and Rosen used the theory of relativity to make this concept of a wormhole. Even a wormhole called the Bifrost bridge in Thor movies is also a type of Einstein-Rosen bridge. Before both Einstein and Rosen, this thing was discovered by Ludwig Flamm (an Austrian physicist) in 1916, just right after Schwarzschild published his solution (Schwarzschild metric).

Like any object or thing, the wormhole also has different parts or sections divided to understand them much better. These parts are as follows:

The mouth of a wormhole: The mouth of the wormhole is the way to enter the wormhole and reach the other point (any location in space).

The long tunnel/throat of a wormhole: The throat or the tunnel-like structure of the wormhole is the inside part of the wormhole which connects the two locations in space.

(Disclaimer: all of the above information about wormhole parts may or may not exist or be properly described, but it is written in a way to help the reader understand wormholes much better.)

The black-white wormhole theory:

As I said before, black holes and white holes are both similar things but with opposite properties. Black holes suck any matter/object inside of it, whereas white holes exert any sort of thing or matter outside of it. As per this, many scientists have said that both black holes and white holes combined to form wormholes. This theory at a point sounds non-realistic, but it makes sense as black holes are objects that suck objects inside of them, which act as an entrance for wormholes. Whereas white holes exert or send out objects from themselves into the vast reaches of space, which acts as the exit way for the wormholes. This theory may sound cool, but it is not confirmed yet whether this is true or not as there is no proper evidence for the existence of wormholes and white holes.

CHAPTER FOUR

The Two Pillars of Physics

Reading the title of this chapter, you might think that what are the pillars of physics, and what does it even mean? Well for you to know, the pillars of physics are Quantum Mechanics and the theory of Relativity. Without both of these theories, the current technology that we have like technology for making electronic devices, satellite communication, and the precise location of an object in space would not have existed, and most importantly without these theories, we would continue to think as time being uniform in space all the time.

- Relativity:-

This is the most well-known and respected theory amongst people who work in the field of physics and science is the theory of Relativity. The theory of Relativity is given and made by Albert Einstein in the 20th Century. This theory is divided into two parts, special and general relativity. The theory of general relativity in short talks about what gravity is in reality. The people who lived before the 20th century thought of gravity as a mysterious force that pulls things and objects in space but then later on Einstein comes along with his grand theory that says that no, gravity is not a mysterious force that everyone had thought of. The theory goes on by saying that gravity is created or is a result of the curvature of spacetime caused due to the mass of a planet or a body present in space.

Illustration of the curvature of spacetime with spacetime here being in 2-dimensional form

Before continuing I would like to clear out the difference between mass and weight. Mass is defined as the quantity of matter in an object or thing while weight is defined as mass multiplied by the pull of gravity acting upon the object.

The theory of special relativity talks about light, matter, and time. A quick example of the theory of special relativity can be imagined as a person throwing and catching plastic balls in the air while you are moving in a car that is going at a speed due to which you can observe the ball going up and down in the air. While you are sitting around and looking at the person in your moving car, you may see the ball going up and down but with a twist that is the ball seems to turn left with up and down motion. You may be confused that how is this possible, the reason is simple and that is due to the frame of reference of the person throwing the balls and you, who is going in a moving car. For the person, the ball is going only up and down while for you who is in a car moving in the leftward direction of the person will of course find the ball going up and down as well but with the ball turning to the left and landing in the person's hand again and again. The theory is not only about the differences in reference frame but also talks about things such as light and time:-

1. Light has a finite speed that is 3 multiplied by 10 raised to the power of 8 and moves at that speed in a vacuum.
2. Time is not the same in space or the observable universe due to different factors. One of these factors can be Gravitational Time Dilation which says that time slows down due to the influence of gravitational force.
3. The speed of light cannot be exceeded as the speed of light is the ultimate constant. It is said that even if you are traveling at the speed of light, the speed of light will still exceed you in speed, unless and until we make fiction come into play.

• Quantum Mechanics:-

Quantum Mechanics is the theory in which we talk about particles and things that are tiny and cannot be seen easily with our naked eyes. Quantum mechanics unlike relativity is quite confusing for most people because it has theories that make the whole theory seem boring and not that easily understandable.

In this book, I shall tell you about this theory in such a way that it is understandable for you, the reader who is currently reading the book. The theory mainly talks about how atoms behave and how things behave at tiny levels that we can't see. Speaking of what is the use of this theory, then well it is that it helps us to create technologies like mobile phones and electronic devices as every electronic device has one thing in common which is the transistor. Quantum mechanics also enables us to have technologies like lasers, MRI (magnetic resonance imaging), electron microscopes, etc.

CHAPTER FIVE

Antiparticles

Before I start telling you about anti-particles, I must inform you about particle physics and what is a particle.

To start, particles are very small localized things or bodies that vary or differ like subatomic particles, macroscopic, microscopic things, etc. These particles can be protons, electrons, photons, neutrons, gas particles, normal dust, etc. Whereas particle physics is a branch of physics that studies particles that comprise radiation and matter.

When a particle or an atom has both its normal state and its anti or opposite-state, it is called an antiparticle. These antiparticles are very rare and yes, they can be created in labs like antimatter. When a particle-antiparticle is mixed or combined, they annihilate themselves and create a form of energy or particle, called a photon.

Some of these antiparticles have similar properties and characteristics. One of these types of antiparticles can be an antihydrogen atom (an antimatter counterpart of hydrogen), which has the same characteristics or properties as a normal hydrogen atom.

One more interesting fact is that these antiparticles can not be created naturally in our world, but they can be created with the help of machines or can be created in special laboratories that can help create these types of particles/atoms.

As said on page 15, antiparticles and anti-atoms can and have been created in labs for the last 50 years. One of these companies which have made antiparticles/anti-atoms for the last 50 years is

CERN. They made the first artificial anti-atom in 1995. Well, you may ask how we can create antiparticles artificially. The answer is that we use big. Powerful and special machines and laboratories for creating antiparticles and anti-atoms. Unlike anti-matter which is very hard to contain or hold, antiparticles and anti-atoms can easily be contained and stabilized.

Anti-particles could be used for various purposes in the future. For example, propulsion for various types of rockets, spacecraft, probes, planes, etc.

Anti-particles can be created now, but soon, they could help us create different sorts of things that we could never imagine in our life. Both anti-particles and anti-atoms are big projects that scientists don't want to leave.

(Hypothetical:- It is said that a particle that can travel faster than the speed of light is called Tachyon. But in reality, it has not yet been confirmed)

CHAPTER SIX

Matter

As we all know, everything which has mass or a thing that takes space by having a certain volume is called matter. To make it simpler, the matter is all around us in different forms, like books, tables, cupboards, laptops, etc.

We have all heard about this topic at least once or twice in our lifetime. But in this book, I would tell you about the matter which is far from any school science textbook or book related to science.

In this chapter, I will tell you about different types of matter, like Dark matter, Antimatter, Mixed matter, Exotic matter, etc.

Dark Matter:

It is a type of matter which makes galaxies stay in shape and it is the matter that holds or keeps stars or solar systems in place rather than swirling out into space. This matter is almost 25% to 27% in total. This makes this matter far more abundant than normal matter, which is only 5%. Let us say that we have a normal matter, which creates gravity stronger than anything. But even this gravity created by the curvature formed by normal matter is not enough or strong enough to hold galaxies and other things in space.

We can also say that, because of this matter, all the things (galaxies, stars, planets, and other astronomical objects) in space are not too close to each other but far from each other. This matter also doesn't reflect or emit light. This is the main reason why scientists have not yet found or seen one. Well, we all know that this matter exists, but in reality, it is very hard to see as it is very complex and its complexity can be made simpler with our current technology or scientific equipment.

You might wonder, "How do we know dark matter exists? When light passes through a few or huge amounts of dark matter at one location, the dark matter bends the light. So from this, we know that there is something that is bending the light and interacting with gravity. Dark matter also has different forms, like mixed dark matter, cold matter, warm matter, baryonic dark matter, etc.

Exotic matter:

As the name says, exotic matter is a type of matter which is exotic, and this matter violates or does not work according to the laws of physics. This type of matter is much rarer and more powerful than we can ever imagine.

The definition which you saw above was just one of the different conclusions and statements about exotic matter. For now, we can say in simple words that exotic matter is a matter which is powerful to even violate the laws of physics.

Antimatter:

As the name says, antimatter is a type of matter which is composed of antiparticles. Antimatter is also said to have two opposite charges, like electron-antielectron (positron) and proton-antiproton. The difference between their normal particle (Eg: electron) and anti-state (Eg: positron) is their charges. Both its anti-state and the normal particle state will have the same amounts of mass, and volume, and takes the same amount of space.

In comparison to regular matter, antimatter is super rare to find in the universe. Not even rare, we can say that it is almost impossible to find in the whole universe.

As for its properties, antimatter is a type of matter that can be super-beneficial for our evolution and boost current technology. Antimatter can be used in the following ways as given below:

- Medical use: antimatter can also be used in different types of medical equipment such as positron emission tomography. Antimatter is also used to eradicate certain types of cancer diseases.

- Fuel and propulsion: This use of antimatter is the most anticipated type of use that scientists, astronauts, and space agencies are looking forward to. If this futuristic technology works, then it would be the most efficient, most powerful, and most useful type of fuel/propulsion ever to be used. If we use antimatter as the fuel of a spacecraft/space probe, it will take much less time and fuel to reach its destination in space.
- For example, let's say that we want to travel to Mars from Earth:
- Scenario 1: If we use normal propulsion or fuel type, it will take us 7 to 8 months to reach the planet.
- Scenario 2: If we use antimatter propulsion or fuel, it will take us only a few months (Around 3 to 4 months or even less).
- Destructive weapons: Well, there is a famous phrase that could tell you about this type of use easily: "If there is peace, some other day there will be wrath". This phrase says that if there is calmness, there will be something that would destroy or end the calmness. This same thing applies to all inventions and creations which we humans have made. For example:
- 4-wheeler automobiles turned into huge battle tanks.
- A normal aircraft/airplane turned into big strategic bombers and fighter planes which bring wrath and devasting consequences to its attack area.

Antimatter has the same fate as the greatest discovery and invention of all time, nuclear and nuclear energy. As with normal nuclear bombs, one antimatter bomb is equivalent to 100 or 1000s of normal atomic/nuclear bombs. When they explode, they emit nuclear and radioactive energy, just like nuclear bombs. But in antimatter bombs, when they explode or burst, they release gamma rays.

You might ask what gamma rays are and why are you so afraid of them so much.

Well, for you, my dear reader, gamma-ray bursts are energy that you would better stay away from. Gamma rays are a type of light that is super powerful. Gamma rays have the shortest wavelength

(Gamma rays = 0.1 Angstroms (The shortest wavelength of light is measured in Angstroms)), which makes it slower to travel long distances and it can only travel short distances than normal light because of this. Also, one more fact, a single gamma-ray burst can destroy a whole planet completely. Just imagine a single antimatter bomb that produces tons and large amounts of gamma rays. A single 'gamma ray' could destroy the entire planet and scientists said that antimatter bombs can produce/burst out tons and huge amounts of 'gamma rays'.

As for now, we can not create any antimatter as it is very costly and dangerous to contain. As per scientists, antimatter is the costliest material to make. Well, every company has different values and estimates for the cost of antimatter. My favorite NASA has said that it would take 62.5 trillion USD per gram of antihydrogen to create/make. As per CERNs, it would cost only a few hundred million Swiss Francs to produce 1 billionth of a gram. Imagine how difficult it would be to create antimatter on our planet at these prices/costs. Well, this was just the cost, but the main reason why this is costly and so difficult to make or create is that we do not have a proper or specific type of technological device which can contain it properly, without annihilating and bursting out huge amounts of gamma rays.

CHAPTER SEVEN

Types of orbits of Earth

Types of orbits of Earth

We are all familiar with the term "orbit" and the various types of planet orbits. But in this chapter, I will be telling you about more advanced types of orbits for Earth orbits, sun-synchronous orbits, transit orbits, escape orbits, etc. I would also tell you about the parts of an orbit in the chapter.

1. LEO (Low Earth orbit): LEO is the smallest orbit around the Earth, that a satellite can revolve around. This is also the most congested orbit of all as this orbit has millions of space debris as compared to other orbits. The advantage of this orbit is that it is very easy to get and make an orbit around the planet as it is closer than other earth orbits. The orbit's altitude ranges from 160 km to 2,000 km. Also, 80% to 90% of satellites/spacecraft revolve or orbit around LEO. As this orbit is nearest to the planet, the signal and radio transmission is much faster and higher than compared radio transmissions/signals of MEO and GEO.

2. PSO (Polar orbit): As the name says, this is a type of orbit where spacecraft/space equipment can be placed to revolve around. This is located at LEO and, as LEO, this orbit has an altitude of 160 km to 2,000 km. The thing which makes this orbit special and different from normal LEO is that the spacecraft in this orbit doesn't revolve around the equator of the planet, but revolves around the poles (North and South poles) of the planet.

3. MEO (Medium Earth orbit): This is also a type of orbit that is located near the earth, but far compared to the LEO. This orbit is rarely used, and spacecraft are rarely launched to orbit it. As compared to LEO's 160 km to 2,000 km altitude, MEO's altitude is much higher, between 2,000 km and 35,786 km.

4. GEO (Geosynchronous Earth orbit): This is the biggest and the highest orbit which can be made around the Earth. Most powerful satellites are placed around this orbit to send signal/ radio transmissions to the whole country. The altitude of GEO is much higher than both MEO and LEO, around 36,000 km.

5. Graveyard orbit: After the service time of the satellite or when its use is completed and not required anymore, it is discarded in this orbit. As the name says, graveyard orbit is the orbit where all used or not required satellites stay and are switched off to spin around. The altitude of the graveyard orbit is higher than 36,000 km.

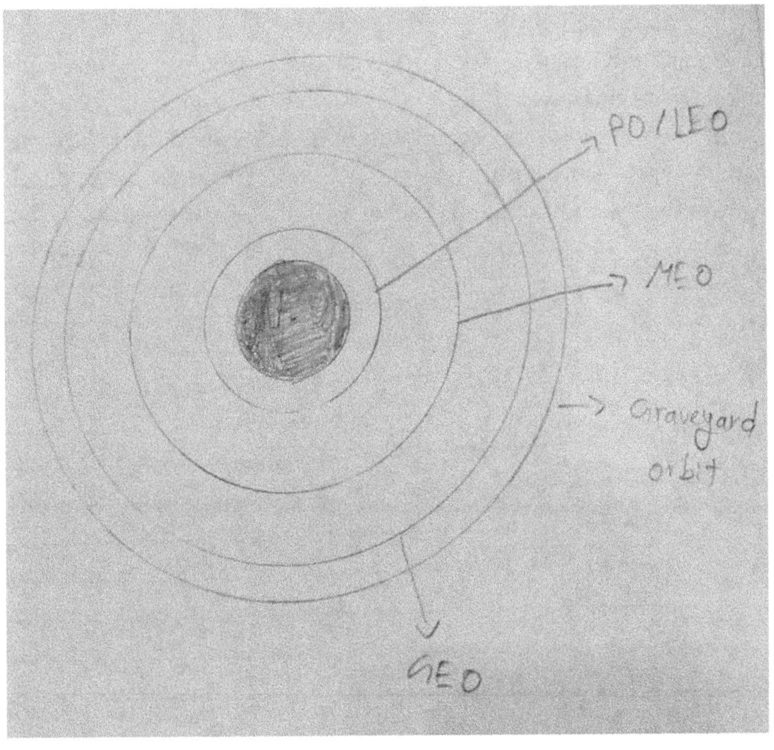

Illustration of different types of orbits

These were just the basic orbits that we can form around our planet, but in real life, there is more to these orbits. As we know, we place or make our satellites and spacecraft revolve around the Earth in other space, but in reality, there's a lot more to just revolving. We all think that space is big and diverse and there's nothing, but in reality, there are a lot of things that we can never imagine and never run away from. One of these things is space debris (For better understanding, we can say that it is space junk created by leftover/ destroyed parts of a spacecraft or multiple spacecraft revolving around Earth). Most of this space debris is caused by us launching rockets, spacecraft, satellites, scientific probes, etc into space and creating a not-so-spacious place for other satellites to come and orbit around the planet.

So as the next generation, it is our responsibility to protect and take care of ourselves. If we humans do not manage space debris, it would be a big mistake because it is quite possible in the future that whenever we launch our rockets from the earth, some space debris may collide with it while the rocket is on the way to its destination.

CHAPTER EIGHT

SI units used in space

As on Earth, we measure with kilometers, meters, centimeters, millimeters, Angstroms, etc. But as the distances in space are very large, it is impossible to use kilometers and meters for long distances. This is why scientists have created two main SI units for calculating very long distances. These distances include Astronomical Units (AU) and Light Years (LY). The astronomical unit is the distance between the Earth and the Sun, which in kilometers is somewhat around 151.94 million kilometers which is quite far in comparison to the distance from Earth to the Moon, For example, Mars is 1.524 AU in comparison to Earth's 1 AU from the Sun.

Light year on the other hand is the distance light travels in one year. Parsec can also be a SI unit that scientists, astronomers, and astrophysicists use to find distances between two objects or things that are further from each other. Light year as I have said is the distance light travels in a year but Parsec on the other hand is 3.261 times a light year.

Here is the conversion:

1 AU (Astronomical unit) = 151.94 million kilometers

1 Light year (LY) = 9.4 trillion kilometers

1 Parsec = 3.26 Light year

As you have read above, I have mentioned something called 'Angstrom' or 'Angstroms'. This word is the metric unit for measuring objects smaller than nanometers. This is mostly used to calculate different wavelengths of light.

Here is the conversion:
1 Angstrom = 0.00000010 cm
or
1 Angstrom = 0.1 nanometers

Satellites

As we near the end of this book, I'd like to tell you about how satellites work and how they've aided us.

Before telling you how satellites work and perform, I would like to tell you about what. In simple words, satellites are man-made objects which are sent to space for better communication, radio transmission, research, exploration, observation, etc. The other meaning of satellites which we all have heard is an astronomical body or celestial body which revolves around a planet, star, or celestial body.

In this chapter, I would tell you about both meanings and explain them in a manner that you will understand.

In space, it is hard to launch different rockets, spacecraft, satellites, and probes because of different forces pulling us down to Earth and not letting us leave the planet's surface. One of these forces is gravity. Unlike regular vehicles for traveling short distances, satellites are more durable, stronger, and heavily protected with coverings of different metals to keep them survivable in the extreme temperatures and forces of space.

Metals and parts used in satellites:

1. Like normal transport and military vehicles, satellites are designed much more accurately to survive in space and some are even designed to return to Earth after going into space. One of the key features in their design is the use of metals for protection against harsh temperatures and forces in space. You might think

that, of course, it will be titanium because it is very strong and it is impossible to even make a crack in the object if it is made up of titanium. Well, for you, my reader, titanium is a great material for protecting objects in space. But in reality, titanium is more expensive than any metal found on the planet Earth. The main reasons why titanium is very expensive are because it is difficult to mine and difficult to find one. Titanium is not the rarest metal found on the planet, but it is much more scarce than steel and copper. This is why many scientists thought of using a metal that is light, durable, and can survive harsh temperatures in space. After long discussions and research, most scientists came up with a conclusion of using either of these two metals, aluminum, and kevlar. These metals also help in attenuation in space.

2. Here is some information about both of these metals:

3. Aluminum: aluminum is the best metal that scientists have found to use in satellites and artificial space vehicles. This metal is much cheaper than titanium and is much lighter compared to titanium. Yes, it is not as strong and durable as titanium, but it is enough to survive in space. Using aluminum also reduces cost and makes launching various spacecraft cheaply and in an affordable manner. Titanium costs 15.00 USD to 30.00 USD per lb. But whereas aluminum costs from 0.15 USD to 0.30 USD per lb. (1 lb (pound) = 0.453592 kg or 1 kg = 2.26 lb). In most satellites, aluminum-coated polyimide is used to cover the satellite and spacecraft. This gives the satellite/spacecraft its iconic golden look and covering. This golden covering or coat is polyimide which protects the spacecraft, space probe, or satellite from thermal energy and heat. We can also say that it acts as an insulator for thermal heat.

4. Kevlar: Kevlar is a type of metal that is mostly used to make bulletproof armor and vests for different countries' policemen/policewomen and armies. This metal is perfect for use in space because of its lightweight, durability, and strong protection. Unlike aluminum, kevlar is a bit expensive to purchase and use. 1 pound of kevlar costs around 2.85 USD. This doesn't mean

that it is better to buy aluminum, but kevlar's high protection is much better compared to aluminum. Kevlar is ideally used for dangerous missions in outer space as it can protect the space vehicle from tiny to huge space debris found revolving around the Sun and Earth.

This was just about the metals that are commonly used by space agencies for their satellites and their space vehicles. There are also other metals like steel and stainless steel which can survive in outer space, but the information I gave you above was about the metals and metal coverings used for most of the satellites and space vehicles. Now let me tell you about how satellites perform and are used for:

Parts of a satellite:

1. Covering: The most important and delicate part of the satellite is its covering and the material used for its covering. These materials are mostly highly durable and strong metals like aluminum, kevlar, titanium, stainless steel, etc.
2. Energy source: energy is the thing because every single machine works. This energy source is either nuclear or electrical. In most cases for satellites, an electric or electrical power source is used as an energy source to keep the craft working and complete its task successfully. Electrical energy is the most efficient and cheaper to add and use in any object as an energy source. Combined with solar panels, these satellites and space crafts work for more than 5 years with no additional removable and recharging of the battery used in the craft. In the case of nuclear-powered crafts and satellites, they are much more expensive to integrate and add because of the batteries. But in the case of nuclear batteries, they provide much more power and energy compared to solar panel electrical batteries and solar batteries. Nuclear-powered batteries work for more than 10 years. Two examples of a space rover that is powered by a nuclear battery are the latest 2020 Perseverance rover and 2011 the Curiosity

rover on Mars. Nuclear-powered spacecraft have long mission periods and having a nuclear reactor on board a satellite or a spacecraft enables the craft to have a longer time to work as even without sunlight or solar panels, it would have more than sufficient amount of energy required to operate. These crafts mostly use Plutonium or Plutonium 238 which is a metal that is radioactive just like Uranium. Normal nuclear-powered plants on the planet use Uranium 238 and Uranium 235 for use and they are quite efficient. The countries that have used nuclear-powered space crafts are Russia and the United States of America.

3. Communication: Let us say that you are in outer space with a nuclear battery to power your craft and an aluminum-coated polyimide covering around your spacecraft, but you aren't able to communicate with anyone in space and back on Earth. Thus, this is why in-space communication is a must. Without communication, we can not get whatever data the craft has sent to us or whatever instructions we want to give to them. The most common way satellites communicate with the ground station is through transmitting data through light in different types. These types can be radio waves, microwaves, infrared radiation, etc. There are certain parts by which satellites and all space vehicles contact the ground station. Such parts are called antennas or large disc-shaped antennas. A normal satellite has two main antennas for communication, the high-gain antenna, and the low-gain antenna. Both of these antennas have different uses and characteristics but work for the same thing; communication.

4. Scientific equipment: Without any sort of scientific equipment, no spacecraft or man-made space vehicles can perform experiments or find much more information about the planet. Most of this scientific equipment is strong enough to survive in space, whereas some are very fragile and can not survive in space without an outer layer of protection. Some of this scientific equipment are IR spectrometers, UV spectrometers, cameras designed for space and deep space, IR radiometers,

magnetometers, plasma wave detectors, spectrographs, etc. Some of these notable space vehicles which had scientific equipment are Hubble Space Telescope, Chandrayaan 1 and 2, Voyager 1 and 2, Parker Solar Probe, New Horizon, the recently launched James Web Space Telescope, etc.

5. Propulsion system: Many of you might have thought about how satellites move around in other spaces and how they can reach other celestial bodies so quickly and easily. Well, for you reader, all spacecraft or any vehicle have legs or wheels to move them. Jet propulsions work on the principle of pushing back the air in front of them at high speeds and at a level through which it can provide lift to the craft that has wings or is aerodynamical. But in outer space, it is impossible to use wheels or normal jet engines as there is no atmosphere or proper flat surface in space. This is why space agencies use liquid, solid, and sometimes ionized engines for space travel and deep space travel. Even these liquid and solid propulsion engines have different variants, depending on the mission's requirement. For example, for normal space exploration to the near celestial bodies we use liquid propulsion, whereas for long deep space exploration we use another type of propulsion like antimatter and nuclear engines. Till now, only liquid, solid, and nuclear propulsion are possible to use and work. But soon, we will have antimatter propulsion systems/ engines.

Uses of satellites in space:
As explained in communications, satellites help us to communicate with ground stations easily, and provide network and transmission to larger areas as compared to ground communication networks. Satellites are also cheaper to send to space and explore planets than sending human-rated crafts to space for billions of dollars. Satellites also help us observe certain things on Earth, like weather, climate, temperature, and even disaster attacks. Some satellites are modified to provide ground support and land coverage to certain countries like China, Russia, the USA, India, Japan, etc.

Satellites can also be used for survey gathering. For example, if a country's government wants to know what all resources their country has or what is the topographic and geographic composition of their nation, they can easily find it using instruments on a satellite. Satellites can also be used to detect resources that can be used by the nation for trade and development of their nation. After all, resources are the backbone of a country and without resources, a country cannot progress more efficiently in comparison with the rest. Satellites can also be used for surveillance over a particular region of a nation like the borders of a country. Speaking of surveillance over the regions of the country's defense, satellites can also be used for warfare purposes like gathering information about the enemy's base, and satellites can be used to monitor an enemy country's movement secretly already without letting them know.

CHAPTER TEN

Extras

Well, for the reader, the book has come to an end, but science is much bigger than we can ever imagine. This is why I have added extra things and subjects related to science and some MCQs that could help you understand whether you have read the book perfectly and understood (optional).

Basic metric conversions:

Mass: Kilogram = (kg) / Gram = (g) / Tonne = (t)

Length: Kilometer = (km) / Meter = (m) / Centimeter = (cm)

Volume: Gallon = (g) / Litre = (l) / Milli-litre = (ml)

Energy: Kilojoule = (kj) / Joule = (j) / Erg = (erg)

Power: Kilowatt = (kW) / Watt = (W) / erg/s

Speed velocity: km/s, m/s, cm/s

Acceleration: m/s2, cm/s2, Gal

Pressure: Pascal = (Pa) / Pieze = (Pz) / Barye = (Ba)

Force: Newton = (n) / Dyne = (dyn) / Sthene = (sn)

Viscosity (μ): Pa.s / Poise (P) / Pz.s

Time: second / hour / nanosecond

Many of us tend to think that space science and science are the only main part of it. But it is wrong, as science is never meant to be limited and it was always meant to discover new things and their properties for understanding.

In astronomy, we have different parts, but these are the main ones:

--> Astrophysics

--> Astrobiology

--> Astrochemistry
--> Astronomy
--> Astrometry
--> Astrobotany
--> Cosmology
--> Planetary science

All of these parts of science or the main parts of astronomy help us understand our universe and the world beyond it clearly and understandably.

Meanings:

1. Density: density is the quantity of mass per unit volume of a substance or matter.
2. Entomology: entomology is the study of insects
3. Hypothesis: a hypothesis is the explanation of a proposed idea or thought.

Facts that you might not know:

1. Comets are leftovers from the creation of different planets, moons, etc. These comets are mostly made out of dust, ice, rock, and different substances.
2. As we talk about junk on land, air, and water, there is junk in space as well. This junk is also called 'space debris. More than 1 million floating space debris of different parts of various non-reusable rockets, satellites, and even space probes meant to leave the planet and research on different planets, moons, and asteroids.
3. The sunset on Mars appears blue instead of orange, or light red on Earth.
4. There are more astronomical objects in the universe than grains of sand or wheat on our planet.
5. Mars has the largest volcano, as far as we know.

6. Europa, Ganymede, Enceladus, and Titan are moons of 2 supermassive gas giants in our solar system which may support life.

As I said before, there's something beyond our planet and our thoughts about space and the universe. There is something more to just the universe and us, there is something more which we will eventually find and get their answers or find them to get our answers. Finally, I'd say that the universe is nothing compared to what we haven't seen yet and may discover in billions of septillions of years.

Well for now we must and should preserve whatever we have caused in the near future we might even not have what we see or think.